CW01304325

RED RACER BOOKS

Presents

ABCs of INDYCAR Racing

My First Guide to INDYCAR® Racing

Written by Andy Amendola

Illustrated by Wei Ren

www.RedRacerBooks.com

For the Fans

Published by Red Racer Books

Copyright © 2023 Red Racer Books LLC.

All rights reserved.

No portion of this book may be reproduced, stored in a retrieval system, or transmitted in any form by any means – electronic, mechanical, photocopy, recording, or other – except for brief quotations in printed reviews, without prior permission of the author.

Hardcover ISBN: 979-8-3507-2109-6

Brickyard, INDYCAR, INDYCAR SERIES, INDY NXT, Indy 500, Indianapolis Motor Speedway (IMS), IMS logos, and IMS landmark IP are all registered trademarks of Brickyard Trademarks, LLC.

RED RACER

Hello Boys and Girls!

Meet Red Racer. He loves all things that go fast. When he was a kid like you, he fell in love with cars. So his papá showed him the world of motorsports, and now he's an excellent race car driver.

Meet Roxy the Engineer! She's Red Racer's partner in racing. Growing up, she loved math and cars. So she studied engineering and aerodynamics. Now she's part of the Red Racer Team, helping to get the best performance from the car.

Join us as we explore the amazing world of the NTT INDYCAR® SERIES! It's a great sport with cool technology, innovative science, and exciting competition.

Vamos! Let's go!

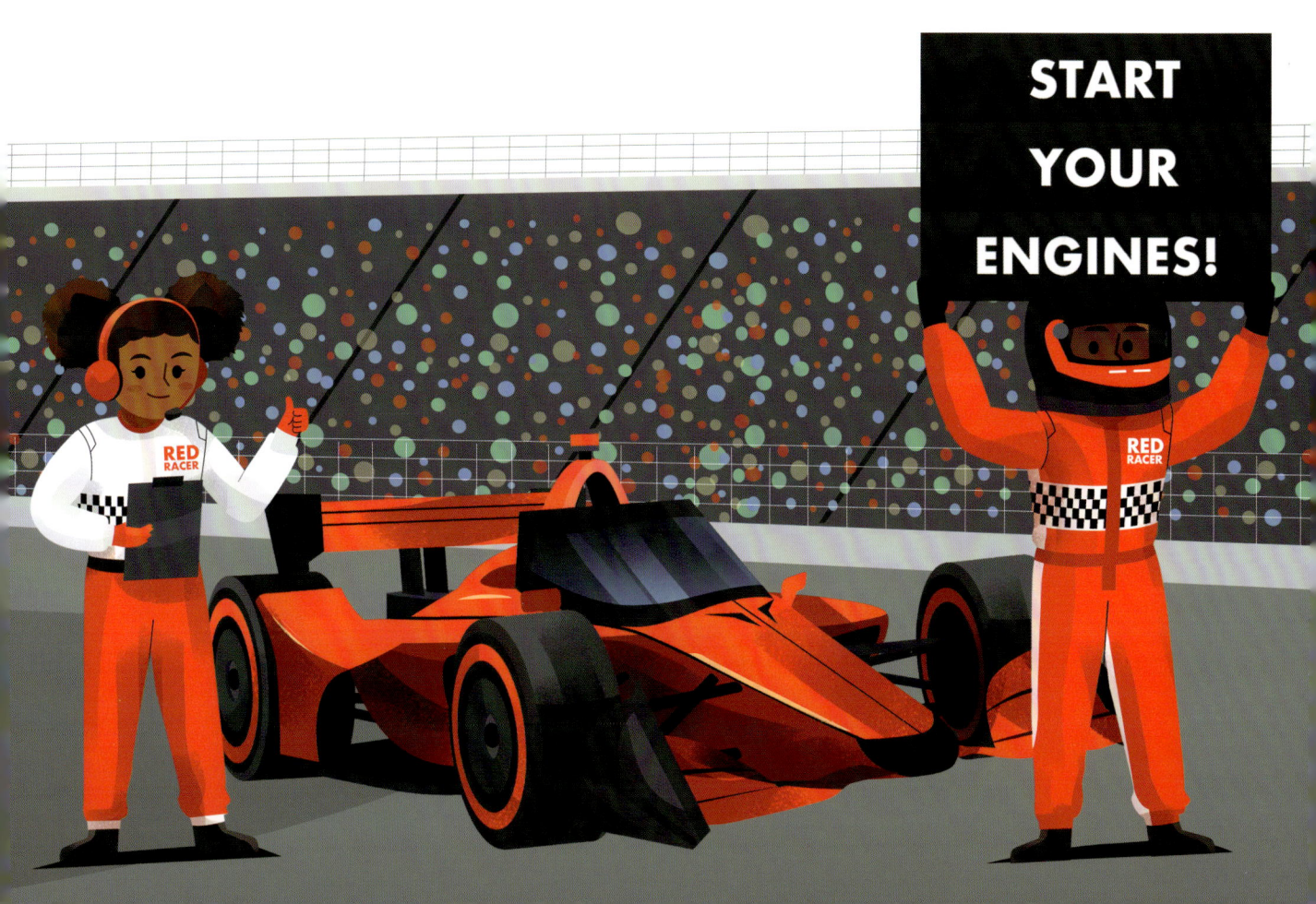

A is for Aeroscreen

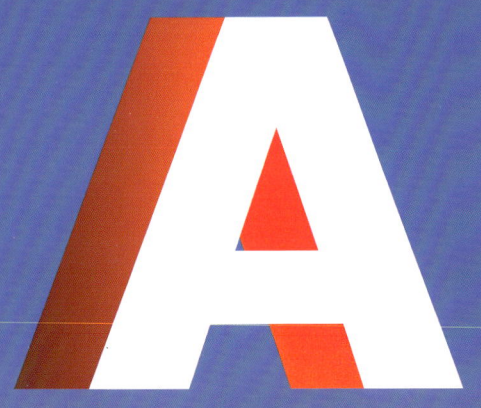

The aeroscreen is a protective window around the drivers. This keeps them safe while driving at speeds up to 240 miles per hour. That aeroscreen is made from the same material used in fighter jets. Wow!

B is for Brickyard

The original track at the world-famous Indianapolis Motor Speedway in Indiana was made with 3.2 million bricks! That's why many call it 'The Brickyard.' Over the years, those bricks were covered with a smooth surface for better racing. But a single yard of bricks remains at the start-finish line. *Imagine how many cars have raced over those bricks!*

C is for Chassis

Vehicles have a chassis ("chaa-see"), which is a frame that holds the car together. It's kind of like the car's skeleton. All INDYCAR race cars use the same kind of strong chassis, which keeps everything together while racing at super high speeds. That's tough stuff!

D is for Drafting

When two cars race really close together, it's called drafting. Cars that are drafting during a race go faster and use less energy than one car alone. That's because the front car blocks the air for the cars behind, giving them all a speed boost. This is thanks to the science of aerodynamics, or how air moves around things. This is a big deal in racing because teams are always looking for ways to go faster!

E is for Engineers

Engineers are an important part of every race team because they help design, build, test and prepare race cars. The INDYCAR SERIES competes at many different types of tracks. So engineers, drivers and their race strategists work together to set the cars up for each new race.

F is for Fuel

Some cars run on electricity, and some use gasoline. But INDYCAR SERIES race cars run on a new fuel made from ethanol that is 100% renewable and causes less pollution. This makes racing better for the planet. Woo-hoo! These cars can stop and add more fuel during pit stops. Then, the team sprays the car with water to prevent fires, and off they go!

G is for G-Forces

When race car drivers accelerate or go around corners, they feel G-forces. The letter "G" stands for gravity, the force that keeps us grounded. Race car drivers can feel up to five times the normal gravity pushing on them while rounding corners. These men and women must be mentally strong and physically fit!

H is for Horsepower

Horsepower (HP) is how we measure the power of an engine. For cars, an engine with higher HP means more power and more speed! In the USA, speed is measured in miles per hour or MPH. INDYCAR SERIES cars have engines with 700 HP that go up to 240 MPH. That's way above the speed limit. Don't try this at home!

is for Indy 500

Short for the Indianapolis 500, this race is a competition of 200 laps around an oval speedway that totals 500 miles. Each Memorial Day weekend, drivers and fans from all over the world attend the Indy 500. This important race has existed for over 100 years. It is one leg of the famed "Triple Crown" of motorsports, alongside the F1 Monaco Grand Prix and the 24 Hours of Le Mans. To date, only one person, Graham Hill, has won all three. Maybe you can be next?

J is for Jumpsuit

In car racing, drivers wear jumpsuits to help keep them safe from fires. Many people call them "fire suits." This one-piece suit covers the whole body, except the head, hands, and feet. It fits pretty tight, but that's for safety, not style. Jumpsuits were first worn by airplane pilots and people who "jumped" from planes with parachutes. Isn't it cool that race car drivers and pilots have so many things in common? *Muy interesante!*

K is for Kiss

Remember that last yard of bricks that remains at the historic Indianapolis Motor Speedway? Every Indy 500 winner and their team gets down onto that track and kisses those bricks. "Kissing the Bricks" is a tradition reserved for those who win at this epic racetrack.

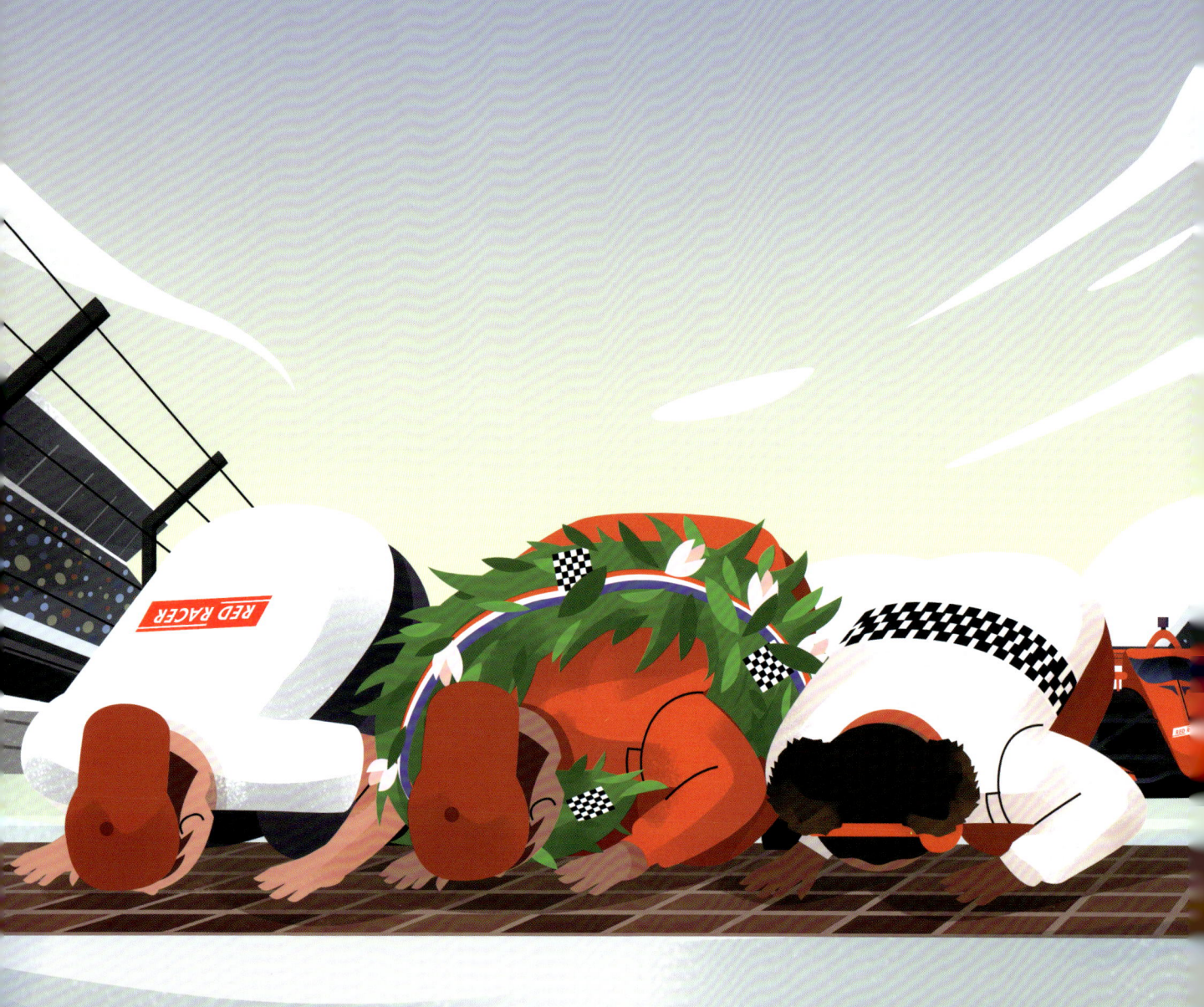

L

is for "Ladies and Gentlemen Start Your Engines!"

Before an INDYCAR SERIES race begins, someone announces the world-famous words, "Start your engines!" Many years ago, only men competed in the races. So they said, "Gentlemen…" When women started racing, they said, "Ladies and gentlemen…" Today, they say, "Drivers, start your engines!" Try this the next time you climb into the car!

M is for Milk

Unlike other races where drivers drink champagne to celebrate victory, winners of the Indy 500 drink a big bottle of milk! It's a treasured tradition dating back over seventy years. The drivers can choose which kind of milk they want! What type of milk would you drink if you won the Indy 500?

N is for NXT

INDY NXT (pronounced 'next') is a junior racing series for young men and women who want to learn skills before joining the professional INDYCAR SERIES. Many superstar drivers have completed this program, which allows kids 16 years and older to race. It's a great way to train the NEXT generation of young talent!

O is for Ovals

INDYCAR races take place on 3 types of tracks: oval shaped circuits, permanent tracks at road courses, and temporary street circuits that pop up around cities. Oval racetracks have been part of American racing since the beginning. Unlike the other types of tracks, which have a mix of right and left turns in each lap, a race on ovals means cars turn in just one direction - left. That makes these tracks extra challenging, with drivers going full speed the entire race!

P is for Push to Pass

A cool feature of INDYCAR racing is push to pass. This is a button on the steering wheel that drivers can press during a race for an extra boost of horsepower. Drivers only get this boost for a limited time, so they must use it wisely! Push to pass is allowed on road and street courses, but not on ovals…yet.

Q is for Qualifying

Qualifying sessions happen before every race. This is how the starting order is set for all the drivers on Race Day. On street circuits and road courses, cars are split into groups, and each driver tries to set the fastest lap time over several rounds. Qualifying is similar on ovals, but cars go one at a time. Either way, the fastest driver in qualifying gets "pole position," meaning he or she is lined up in the very front at race time.

R is for Rolling Start

INDYCAR races begin with a rolling start, meaning the cars are already moving before the race begins. In a rolling start, all drivers complete at least one lap where all cars are moving together. They move in rows of 2s or even rows of 3s, like in the Indy 500. When the green flag waves, the drivers take off!

S is for Safety Team

The safety team travels to every INDYCAR race to help drivers when accidents happen. Within seconds of a crash, they arrive with a truck full of tools to fight fires and to help drivers get out safely. These men and women are heroes who keep our favorite drivers safe. Wave and say "thanks" to the safety team next time you see them.

T *is for Tires*

Race cars use tires called "slicks." They are different from regular tires and are all smooth, with no grooves! Teams choose from two types of tires: "primary tires" are all black, and "alternate tires" are chosen according to the track, appearing with red or green bands. In rainy conditions, teams can use special "wet tires" with grooves to prevent slipping and sliding. This doesn't apply to oval races, where teams use just one type of tire and racing stops when it rains.

U is for Umbrellas

In racing, umbrellas aren't used just for rain! They can be used to give drivers shade as they sit in their cars waiting for a race to start, especially in the heat of summer. *Caliente!* The temperature on the track gets much hotter than the air because most tracks are made from a material that absorbs heat. *Talk about hot wheels!*

V is for V6

You can hear an INDYCAR's loud, powerful engine from far away. All race cars must use the same type of engine called a V6. It's called a V6 because the engine is shaped like a "V" and has six cylinders, three on each side, plus a twin turbo. And now, hybrid technology is being added for even more speed. Vroom! Vroom!

W is for Wings

Like planes, race cars have wings. But planes use wings to help them lift up off the ground. Race cars use wings to push them down to the ground. Wings at the front and the back of these cars create downforce while racing at high speeds. This helps the cars grip the track and go even faster, especially around turns. But each track is different, so teams change wings depending on the type of track.

SPEEDWAY

ROAD COURSE

RED RACER

X is for eXciting!

Few words start with "X," but INDYCAR racing is super eXciting. Daring drivers, high-tech cars, and teams of people all work together to win a race that may come down to the last second. It's so fun to see, including the celebrations afterwards! Woo-hoo!

Y is for Yellow Flag

A yellow flag signals caution and alerts drivers to slow down. It means something has happened on the track that could be dangerous. Many different colors and styles of flags are waved by race officials to communicate with drivers. The flags are an important backup in case radio communication fails. The checkered flag is my favorite!

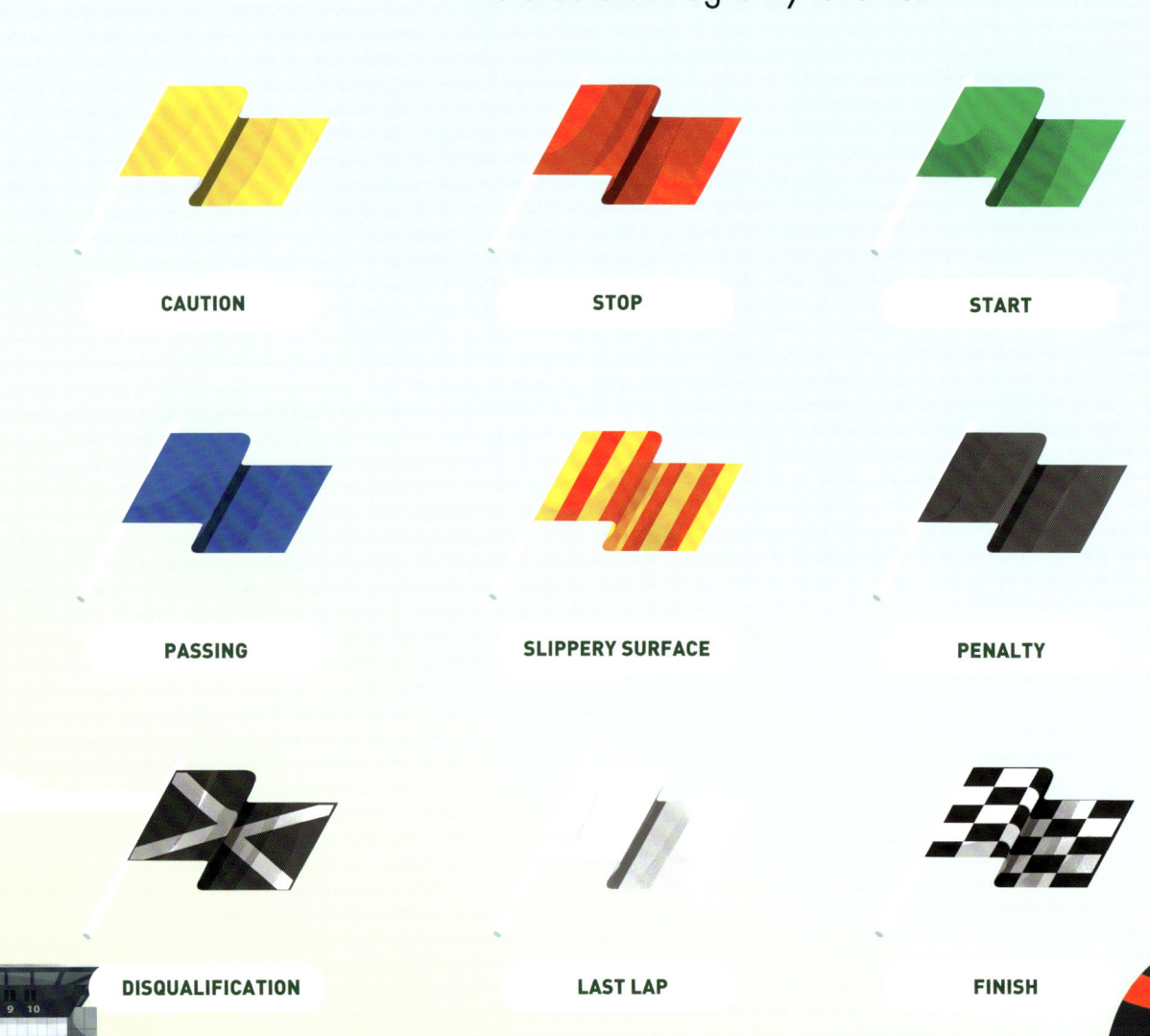

CAUTION	STOP	START
PASSING	SLIPPERY SURFACE	PENALTY
DISQUALIFICATION	LAST LAP	FINISH

Z is for Zoom

Going out to a track to watch a race in person is super fun! The cars are so fast that sometimes all you hear is "Zoom…Zoom…Zoom," with each car that passes by. The engines are so loud you can feel it in your whole body. So, grab something to protect your ears and enjoy an exciting experience at a race near you!

RED RACER

Boys and Girls!

The checkered flag is waving, which means you've crossed the finish line! Bravo! Did you like learning about INDYCAR racing as much as we did?

If you have any questions, suggestions, or want to learn more, ask your parents to find us on social media. Together, you can post and connect with the Red Racer fam directly!

More books coming soon!

Hasta Pronto! That means see you soon.

Red Racer and Roxy out!

ACKNOWLEDGMENTS

This book stands as a tribute to the passion and camaraderie of the racing community. A heartfelt thanks to all the INDYCAR fans, insiders and friends for their insights and encouragement. The input from both you and your kids has truly made this book something special. Thanks for being part of this ride with me.
Happy Reading and Happy Racing!

Contributors

- Daniel Incandela - Indianapolis, IN
- D.J. Fluck - Chandler, AZ
- Erik Richardson - Kokomo, IN

Beta-Testers & Junior Test Drivers Team

- Abigail Thomson-Gagne, Amber Thomson & Nathan Gagne - Montreal, Quebec, Canada
- Addison & Heidi Fluck - Chandler, AZ
- Alex Offenbach - Indianapolis, IN
- Alyssa Ruklic - Crete, Illinois
- Anwar, Amir & Omar Jalife - Mexico City, Mexico.
- Asher, Finnegan, Kristen & Zach Gaddis - Dunkirk, Maryland.
- Calvin, Olsen, and Jared Fields - Kingsland, TX
- Chandler - Altoona, Iowa
- Eddie & Sophie
- Ethan & Henry Incandela - Indianapolis, IN
- Francis, John Paul, Josh Chang and Crystal Ortegon - Austin, TX
- Kali & Logan Aerts - Highland, IN
- Ken Jeffries
- Liam & Oliver Castro - Middlebury, CT
- Lincoln, Preston & Jacob Cleary - Parma, OH
- Logan Richardson - Lansing, MI
- Luke Smith - Coatesville, Indiana
- Marc, Jayce, and Cameron Wynter - Pembroke Pines, FL
- Oscar Cooper & his race driver Dad, Jonny Cooper - Sutton, UK
- Richard Cormack - Adelaide South Australia
- Sebastian and Andrew Zeegers - Calgary Ab. Canada
- Shelby & Lily Hisey - Ohio
- Tom Griffiths - Kent, England
- William & Daniel Young - Portland, OR
- William Staab - Trophy Club, Texas
- Zac & Daniel Carroll - Ashland, VA

Editors

- Becky Ross Michael - Frisco, TX
- Leah Grossman - Miami, FL

Special thanks to Paula and Tatiana Calderón, for continually inspiring children across the world.

Meet The Author - Andy Amendola

Andy, a proud Hispanic American, discovered a deeper love for driving when he encountered motorsports. Eager to share this newfound passion with his kids and the world, he recognized racing's potential to inspire futures. That's why he founded Red Racer Books. Andy lives in Miami, Florida with his wife Angela, their children Blanca and Joaquin, and a pup named Skye.

Meet the Illustrator - Wei Ren

Wei Ren, also a father, resides in Fuzhou, in the Fujian province of China. Originally a UI designer, Wei Ren is a talented artist and painter who has recently ventured into more illustration projects.

About Red Racer Books

Red Racer Books brings the thrill of motorsports to young readers, ages 1-10. We live by 'you can't be what you can't see.' So, our books showcase diverse characters in various racing roles, not just drivers. We highlight the science, teamwork, and diversity in racing. Each book is more than just a sport's intro; it's a call to dream and connect.

Connect with Red Racer online!
Follow us @RedRacerBooks

And Subscribe at www.RedRacerBooks.com
and stay tuned for more books!